ALEX RODRIGUEZ

MARK LANGSTON

RUPPERT JONES

FREDDY GARCIA

JULIO CRUZ

KEN GRIFFEY JR.

BRET BOONE

RANDY JOHNSON

BRUCE BOCHTE

ICHIRO SUZUKI

JAY BUHNER

EDGAR MARTINEZ

THE HISTORY OF THE
SEATTLE
MARINERS

MICHAEL E. GOODMAN

CREATIVE EDUCATION

Published by Creative Education, 123 South Broad Street, Mankato, MN 56001

Creative Education is an imprint of The Creative Company.

Designed by Rita Marshall.

Photographs by AllSport (Stephen Dunn, Otto Greule, Rick Stewart), Icon Sports Media

(John Cordes, Chuck Solomon), Diane Johnson, SportsChrome (Rob Tringali Jr., Michael Zito)

Library of Congress Cataloging-in-Publication Data

Goodman, Michael E. The history of the Seattle Mariners / by Michael Goodman.

p. cm. — (Baseball)   ISBN 1-58341-224-7

Summary: A team history of the Seattle Mariners, a club formed in 1976 with the

awarding of an American League franchise to Seattle.

1. Seattle Mariners (Baseball team)—History—

Juvenile literature. [1. Seattle Mariners (Baseball team)—History.

2. Baseball—History.] I. Title. II. Baseball (Mankato, Minn.).

GV875.S42 G64 2002   796.357'64'09797772—dc21   2001047869

First Edition 9 8 7 6 5 4 3 2 1

THE CITY

OF SEATTLE, WASHINGTON, WAS FOUNDED IN 1851

when 22 settlers landed boats in the area and built homes on the

bluffs overlooking Elliott Bay. More pioneers might have followed

to the Pacific Northwest, but the Civil War and wars with Native

Americans kept most from making the journey. Finally, in the

1880s, westward movement began again, and Seattle quickly grew

into the center of commerce and culture in the region.

In 1977, another group of pioneers—the Seattle Mariners

professional baseball team—established a home in the Pacific

Northwest. They, too, got off to a slow start, taking 15 years to

record their first winning season. But the journey has been upward

in the standings since that time, and the Mariners have grown to

DIEGO SEGUI

become one of baseball's strongest and most compelling franchises, building a loyal following throughout the region.

{FROM PILOTS TO MARINERS} Winning games wasn't the biggest challenge at first for Seattle baseball players and fans. The initial problem was getting and keeping a team. The city's first major-league club, the Pilots, joined the American League (AL) in 1968 but

6 lasted only one season because of money problems. Then, in 1976, the AL awarded a new franchise to Seattle to begin play the next season. Fans eagerly participated in a poll to help name the new franchise. The overwhelming choice was Mariners. It was a perfect name since—next to baseball—boating was the favorite recreation of many Seattle residents.

Excitement built up for the Mariners' opening night in 1977. Manager Darrell Johnson announced that Diego Segui would pitch

JAY BUHNER

Equally sound in the field and at the plate, Bruce Bochte was an early Seattle star.

BRUCE BOCHTE

the new team's first game. Mariners fans were already familiar with the Cuban right-hander since he had also pitched for the Pilots nearly a decade before. Segui and the Mariners suffered a 7–0 loss to the California Angels that night, the first of many tough defeats for the club that season. The Mariners finished the year 64–98, next-to-last in the AL Western Division.

Julio Cruz drove opposing pitchers mad, averaging 41 steals a year during his Mariners career.

Still, fans enjoyed watching the exploits of such players as veteran outfielder Lee Stanton—who smacked 27 home runs and drove in 90 runs—and two rookies, outfielder Ruppert Jones and second baseman Julio Cruz. Jones's outstanding all-around play earned him a spot on the AL All-Star team in 1977 and had Mariners fans yelling "Rupe! Rupe!" each time he came to bat or chased down a fly ball. Meanwhile, the speedy Cruz quickly established himself as one of the AL's top base stealers.

JULIO CRUZ

The beautiful SAFECO Field, which opened in **2000**, has a huge retractable roof.

SAFECO FIELD

{BATTLING BEHIND BOCHTE} In 1978, first baseman Bruce

Bochte joined the team as a free agent and became one of its first

real stars. Bochte opened his first season in Seattle

hitting well above .300. "In the beginning, I was the

only one on the team hitting the ball," he recalled. "It

got to the point that I felt if I didn't get two hits and

drive in two runs, we wouldn't win the game." That

In **1982**, a
Seattle-versus-
California
game went
20 innings
and lasted
more than
six hours.

12 pressure seemed to take a toll on Bochte, and his performance

suffered. By season's end, his average had fallen to .263, and his

slump helped drop the Mariners to a last-place finish at 67–95.

The next season, both Bochte and the Mariners improved.

Bochte batted .316 and posted 100 RBI. He also thrilled Mariners

fans by driving in a run in the 1979 All-Star Game, which was held

in Seattle's Kingdome. With Bochte and designated hitter Willie

Horton providing solid offense from the third and fourth spots in

HAROLD REYNOLDS

the Mariners' lineup, the club finished the season with 11 more wins than it had in 1978.

Bochte had several more fine years for the Mariners. Then,

after the 1982 season, he decided to retire from baseball, explaining that the game was no longer fun for him. Seattle fans were sad to see their first real hero go.

{A MOUND TURNAROUND} While early Mariners teams

featured strong hitting, the club lacked solid pitching. It seemed that

no matter how many runs the offense produced, the

The **1982** season was a nail-biter in Seattle, as 31 of the Mariners' victories came by a single run.

pitchers seemed to give up more. That began to change

in 1982. New manager Rene Lacheman, who was a

former pitching coach, helped the club's best young

hurler, Floyd Bannister, gain better control of his blazing

14 fastball. The lefty responded by leading the league in strikeouts.

Bannister's improvement was only one important pitching

change in 1982. The club also added relief pitchers Bill Caudill and

Ed Vande Berg and signed two-time Cy Young Award winner

Gaylord Perry to bolster the starting staff. Perry, a future

Hall-of-Famer, won his 300th game in a Mariners uniform, and his

10 victories helped Seattle improve to 76–86 in 1982.

Over the next decade, the Mariners continued to rise in the

GAYLORD PERRY

AL standings as they built a solid nucleus of young, talented players.

Two important parts of that nucleus arrived in 1984: hard-hitting

first baseman Alvin Davis and southpaw pitcher Mark Langston.

Davis quickly established himself as the club's top offensive star and

finished the 1984 season with 27 home runs and 116 RBI. Langston

used a great curveball and a blazing heater to become the first rookie in 30 years to lead the AL in strikeouts, fanning 204 batters.

Key injuries pulled Seattle down in 1985 and 1986, but the

Mariners were back and better than ever in 1987,

challenging for the AL West lead for much of the

season. Langston set a club record with 19 wins,

Davis and center fielder Phil Bradley each batted

over .300, and second baseman Harold Reynolds led

the league with 60 stolen bases. A late-season collapse, however,

dropped Seattle to fourth place in the standings behind the

division-winning Minnesota Twins.

Finally, team owner George Argyros became impatient. "The

Mariners are no longer an expansion team," he announced. "It's time

we began winning." Argyros changed managers and made several

strategic trades, shipping off Langston and Bradley and bringing in

promising but unproven players such as pitcher Randy Johnson

Utility player Scott Bradley and the Mariners stole 174 bases in **1987**, setting a club record.

SCOTT BRADLEY

Known to fans as simply "Junior," Ken Griffey Jr. was one of the game's elite stars.

and burly outfielder Jay Buhner, who would play big roles in the team's future.

{A WINNING COMBINATION} The Mariners began the 1990s still looking for their first winning season. But Seattle fans believed that their long wait would soon be over. There were three main reasons for optimism in Seattle—Johnson, outfielder Ken Griffey Jr., and third baseman Edgar Martinez.

The 6-foot-10 Johnson, nicknamed the "Big Unit," came to Seattle in 1989 with a reputation as a hard thrower with little control. Luckily, he learned to limit his wildness, and over the next few seasons he became the most feared pitcher in the AL. Said Texas Rangers manager Doug Melvin, "Randy Johnson has become what [Hall of Fame pitcher] Sandy Koufax was."

Arriving in Seattle in 1989 at the age of 19, "Junior" Griffey

RANDY JOHNSON

quickly proved he could do it all—hit for average and power, drive

in runs, run the bases, and excel at his tough center field position.

"I don't think anybody has ever been that good at that age," said

Mariners batting coach Gene Clines. "He's in his own category."

In 1990, Griffey recorded the first of five straight seasons

batting .300 or better. AL opponents feared the left-handed slugger, but he wasn't the only offensive weapon in the Mariners' arsenal.

Martinez was just as dangerous as Junior and almost as powerful.

Omar Vizquel was the game's best defensive shortstop in **1992**, committing only seven errors. The third baseman began his own .300-plus streak in 1990 and captured AL batting titles in both 1992 and 1995.

Seattle's "big three" and other talented players such as Buhner, shortstop Omar Vizquel, catcher

22 Dave Valle, and pitcher Erik Hanson helped power the team to an 83–79 record in 1991. The Mariners were winners at last!

{PINIELLA HAS THE WINNING TOUCH} A new era in Mariners history officially began on November 9, 1992, when Lou Piniella was hired as manager. The fiery Piniella, a former big-league outfielder and a winning manager in both New York and Cincinnati, brought a new intensity to the Seattle dugout. Piniella drove the Mariners to another winning season in 1993 and then to

OMAR VIZQUEL

Lou Piniella spent 16 seasons in the AL as a player before becoming a manager.

LOU PINIELLA

their first AL West title in 1995.

In the 1995 postseason, the Mariners outbattled the New York Yankees in a classic divisional playoff—which included an exciting come-from-behind victory in 11 innings in game five—to reach the AL Championship Series (ALCS). As usual, the big heroes in game five were Griffey, Martinez, and Johnson. Junior smacked a home run to send the game into extra innings and then scored the winning run on a Martinez double in the bottom of the 11th. Johnson, meanwhile, came into the game in the ninth inning on only one day's rest and shut down the Yankees for the win.

A brilliant hitter, infielder Edgar Martinez put together four 100-RBI seasons in the **1990s**.

When the Mariners won two of the first three games in the ALCS against the Cleveland Indians, Seattle fans began to dream of a World Series championship. Unfortunately, the Indians then swept the next three contests to end the Mariners' magical run.

EDGAR MARTINEZ

In 1996, the Mariners nearly made the playoffs again thanks to an impressive new star: shortstop Alex Rodriguez. In his first full major-league season, "A-Rod" captured the AL batting title with a

.358 average, slugged 36 home runs, drove in 123 runs, scored 143 more, and finished a close second in the voting for AL Most Valuable Player (MVP). "Alex has a good chance to be the best

shortstop ever," said Baltimore's future Hall of Fame shortstop Cal Ripken Jr.

The next year, Griffey earned the AL MVP award with 56 homers and 147 RBI, and Johnson posted a 20–4 record with 291 strikeouts in 211 innings. These performances helped propel Seattle to a club-record 90 wins and another playoff berth. Yet the Mariners fell once again in the postseason, losing to the Baltimore Orioles. "It's always tough to lose," said Rodriguez after the defeat, "but we're still a young team, and I think our time is coming soon."

{BUILDING A NEW CAST} The Mariners stayed near the top of the AL West over the next few seasons, but their roster underwent major changes. One by one, Johnson, Griffey, and Rodriguez all left Seattle via trades or free agency. The club also moved to a new home, leaving the Kingdome in 1999 after 22 seasons for the

Arguably baseball's best all-around player, shortstop Alex Rodriguez stole 46 bases in **1998**.

ALEX RODRIGUEZ

open-air SAFECO Field. Through it all, Piniella kept the Mariners together and winning.

Seattle entered the 21st century with several newcomers on the roster, including starting pitchers Freddy Garcia and Aaron Sele, Japanese rookie closer Kazuhiro Sasaki, outfielder Mike Cameron, and first baseman John Olerud. In 2000, that crew helped the

Mariners earn a wild-card berth in the playoffs, sweep the favored Chicago White Sox, and push the New York Yankees to six games in the ALCS. Sasaki was the year's most pleasant surprise. In his first season playing baseball in America, he set a major-league rookie record with 37 saves and was named AL Rookie of the Year.

In 2001, two new arrivals helped make the Mariners a true powerhouse: veteran second baseman Bret Boone and outfielder Ichiro Suzuki, another major-league rookie with years of experience

FREDDY GARCIA

in Japan. Boone put up MVP-type numbers throughout the season,

finishing with a league-leading 141 RBI, an AL record for second

basemen. Yet even his outstanding play was over-

shadowed by Suzuki's performance. Opening the

season with hits in 46 of the Mariners' first 49 games,

the speedy outfielder stunned even his teammates.

"I'd be lying if I thought he'd be anywhere near this

good," said Mariners outfielder Al Martin.

Suzuki broke the major-league record for hits by a rookie set

in 1911 by the legendary "Shoeless" Joe Jackson. And his defense was

almost as exciting, especially his accurate throws from deep right

field to cut down opposing runners. With a high-powered offense

and outstanding pitching, the Mariners cruised to an AL-record

116 regular-season wins in 2001 and into the playoffs again. Sadly,

things came to a screeching halt in the ALCS as the Mariners were

JOHN OLERUD

Strong-armed
second
baseman
Bret Boone
had the season
of a lifetime
in **2001**.

BRET BOONE

Japanese sensation Ichiro Suzuki was known for his quick feet and sweet swing.

ICHIRO SUZUKI

toppled once again by the Yankees.

It took many years for the Mariners to build a winning

The Mariners faithful expected offensive help from newly acquired third baseman Jeff Cirillo.

combination, but Seattle fans have always shown great

patience and loyalty for their team. Now, with all of

the elements seemingly in place for a long run near

the top of the AL, fans in the Pacific Northwest are

hoping the Mariners will have smooth sailing toward

their first world championship.

JEFF CIRILLO